The Norman Conquest depicted in picture-strip form on the Bayeux Tapestry, a wool-embroidered linen panel, 75 metres (82 yards) long, probably made in Canterbury to the order of Bishop Odo. It starts with Harold's visit to Normandy, where he swears to uphold William's claim to the English throne. Harold insisted the oath was made under duress as a prisoner. The tapestry shows us how the Normans lived, fought and built castles. The early castle at Hastings is being built here.

Normandy itself had been founded by Vikings in 911. Just 150 years later, an army of Normans, descendants of these 'Northmen', prepared to cross the Channel and invade the bigger, richer kingdom of the English. The Norman leader, Duke William, considered the land rightfully his, promised both by his childless kinsman, Edward the Confessor, and by Harold Godwinsson. However, despite any previous vows which may have been made to William, Edward died in January 1066 accepting Harold as his successor, and the English nobles duly elected him king.

— Above —

Built by William I, the White Tower that dominates the Tower of London is the largest and oldest keep in England. Entered at first floor level, like other Norman castles, it had living quarters for the king.

Expecting William's reaction, Harold deployed forces on the south coast, but found himself instead facing invasion from Scandinavia, led by the King of Norway and Harold's own brother, Tostig. Marching swiftly north, Harold won a famous victory at Stamford Bridge, near York. Three days later, a fleet of 700 Norman ships landed at Pevensey on the Sussex coast. Harold wheeled south, spurning delay for fresh reinforcements in favour of speed and surprise.

William's army was waiting. Saxon England fought for its life that autumn Saturday on Senlac Hill. Its foot soldiers stood firm against archers and cavalry, but broke ranks to chase fleeing Normans and were cut to pieces. Harold died at dusk at the foot of his royal standard; his bodyguard, brandishing battleaxes, fought to the last man. After 500 years of Saxon rule in England, invading Norsemen had finally triumphed.

Rule of the Sword

William set out to bend England to his will. To force its surrender he marched his troops around London, slaughtering and burning wherever he met resistance. One by one the cities, churchmen and nobles submitted to their new master. On Christmas Day 1066, the Conqueror was crowned in Edward the Confessor's new abbey at Westminster.

The Saxons had settled in Britain to farm, but the Normans came to rule. A small army of occupation kept control from castles built to act as barracks, watchtowers, forts and administrative headquarters. Castles commanded the landscape and, from these symbols of Norman domination, cavalry patrols rode out to stifle the uprisings and invasions that continued for five years. Though cowed, the Saxons were not yet quelled.

— RIGHT —

Heavy Norman swords were designed to be swung with both hands, which were protected by a guard, or pommel. Blades were straight and double-edged.

— ABOVE —

Norman knights, riding straight-legged, charging into battle with the lance held steady beneath the arm.

— RIGHT —

Pickering Castle, North Yorkshire. Norman castles stood on an earth mound, or motte. On top was a fort and, at the base, a fortified and enclosed bailey. Early motte-and-bailey castles could be built in a fortnight, and by 1100 there were at least 500 in England.

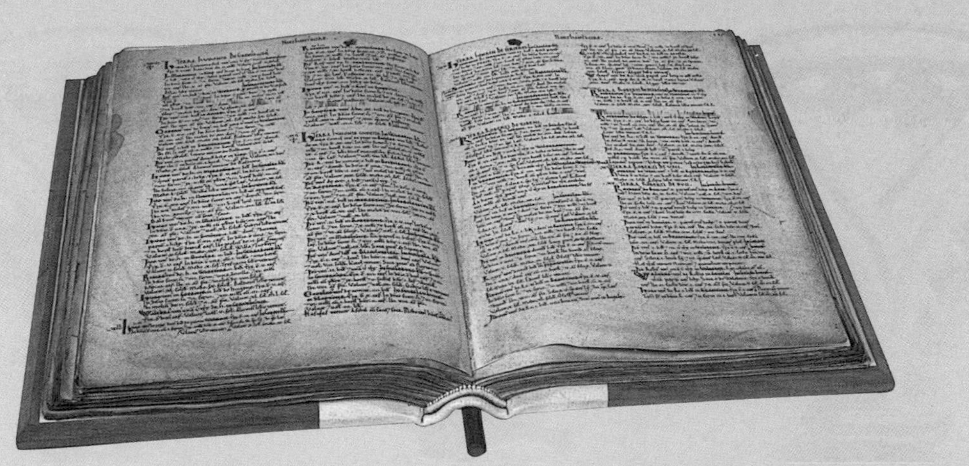

The Domesday Book was so called because, like the Day of Judgement (Doom), none could escape its scrutiny. In 1086, William I sent officials to survey land resources in England. They heard evidence sworn in court by juries of priests, reeves and six men from each village. A typical entry reads: 'In Wallington, Fulco holds of Gilbert 3 hides and 40 acres of land. There is land for five ploughs … There is pasture for beasts and wood for hedges … Altogether it is worth 50s [shillings]. When he received it, 30s. At the time of king Edward, 100s.'

William soon left for Normandy, leaving his half-brother Odo, Bishop of Bayeux, to consolidate the work of conquest. In 1067 William was back to crush revolt at Exeter and in 1069 savagely punished a great northern rebellion. Rebels who had sacked Peterborough Abbey with Hereward the Wake were ruthlessly hunted down but Edric the Wild, leader of resistance on the Welsh borders, was pardoned. Norman retribution was apparently not always merciless. Having completed his conquest of England, William then advanced on Scotland to gain the submission of its king, Malcolm Canmore, in 1072.

— Above —

A peasant's dwelling in Norman times: a reconstruction at the Weald & Downland Museum, Singleton, West Sussex.

Steadily but remorselessly, French-speaking Normans spread through England's government and Church. They already had its land. English land was William's own battle spoil, the reward he shared out to the military chiefs who had helped him win it. They held it as his 'vassals', swearing allegiance and fighting for him when called. Land-holding was the basis of Norman feudalism. The king's land was let to barons; barons let lands to knights and freemen; they in turn let lands to peasants, who worked the lord's land and their own. By the time William ordered the Domesday survey of his kingdom in 1086, some 200 Normans had replaced over 4,000 Saxon landlords.

Builders in Stone

— Left —

The Chapel of St John in the Tower of London. Starkly simple apart from carved capitals on the columns, it is the only keep chapel with aisles and a continuous gallery above.

— Above —

A carved stone capital from the Norman crypt of Canterbury Cathedral.

William had seized England with the Pope's blessing. The Conqueror was a good churchman, proud of the monasteries he had founded: 'While I was duke, seventeen abbeys of monks and six of nuns were built … These are the fortresses by which Normandy is guarded.' Famed for their learning, they attracted the Italian scholars Lanfranc and Anselm who were in turn to be made Archbishop of Canterbury by William and his successor.

William founded his first English abbey at Battle, on the site of his victory. He sought to order the English Church as he had its government, using energetic scholars, administrators, builders and business men from Normandy to modernize a Church whose long-venerated Saxon saints they viewed as 'rustic', and whose abbots they thought 'uncultured idiots'. Lanfranc organized dioceses and cathedral chapters, developed separate Church courts and Church law. He also tried to make a priest's blessing requisite for lawful marriage and to impose celibacy on the priesthood.

— Below —

The vaulted undercroft at Fountains Abbey, Yorkshire, the finest such cellars in Europe.

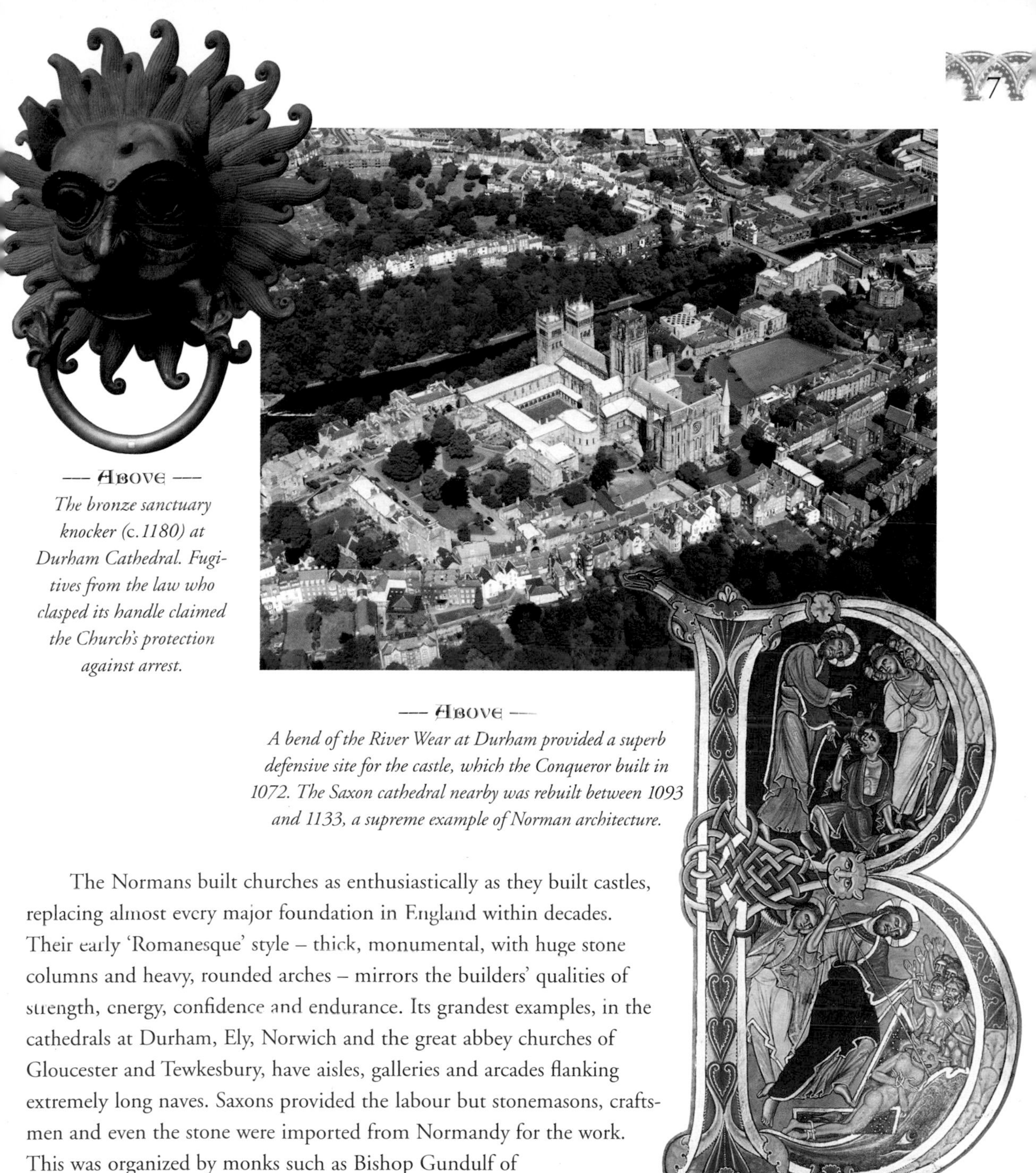

— Above —
The bronze sanctuary knocker (c.1180) at Durham Cathedral. Fugitives from the law who clasped its handle claimed the Church's protection against arrest.

— Above —
A bend of the River Wear at Durham provided a superb defensive site for the castle, which the Conqueror built in 1072. The Saxon cathedral nearby was rebuilt between 1093 and 1133, a supreme example of Norman architecture.

The Normans built churches as enthusiastically as they built castles, replacing almost every major foundation in England within decades. Their early 'Romanesque' style – thick, monumental, with huge stone columns and heavy, rounded arches – mirrors the builders' qualities of strength, energy, confidence and endurance. Its grandest examples, in the cathedrals at Durham, Ely, Norwich and the great abbey churches of Gloucester and Tewkesbury, have aisles, galleries and arcades flanking extremely long naves. Saxons provided the labour but stonemasons, craftsmen and even the stone were imported from Normandy for the work. This was organized by monks such as Bishop Gundulf of Rochester, who rebuilt the cathedral and castle there, and is also credited with designing the White Tower of the Tower of London.

Bishops could wield as much power as barons. Some, like Odo, were barons in their own right, but they also held the Church's lands in trust from the king, swearing fealty and rendering knight service for it. William, however, insisted on mastery of his newly-won kingdom. He refused to do homage to the Pope for it, further declaring that no pope was to be recognized in England without the king's sanction.

— Above —
An illuminated letter from the Winchester Bible, created over a period of 30 years for Henry of Blois (1129–71), Bishop of Winchester and younger brother of King Stephen.

Feudal Feuds

— Above —
The seal of William Rufus portrays the king on horseback, armed for warfare.

William granted land units (fiefs) shrewdly, allocating half of all farmland to the nobles, and a quarter to the Church. The rest he kept for himself. Nobles governed their estates, or manors, for the king from their castles or fortified manor houses. No castle could be built without the king's permission and no baron could keep a private army. In this way William sought to prevent in England wars like those waged between nobles in Normandy. To counterbalance the power of individual barons over their local area, he retained the Saxon system of sheriffs acting on the king's behalf.

William began by confirming the laws of Edward the Confessor and claiming no new prerogatives. He retained Saxon forms of government, and even tried to learn English, but by the end of his reign the Norman flair for adaptation had produced a Normanized administration run by officials with such titles as steward, butler, chamberlain, constable, marshal and chancellor. The chancellor headed the scriptorium, the department issuing royal commands or writs, which were produced at first in English but later in Latin. The Normans themselves spoke Norman French.

Dover Castle, with its massive Norman tower keep, replaced an earlier wooden structure on the old Saxon-Roman fort site. The weight of these immense towers, 30 metres (98 feet) square and with walls up to 7 metres (23 feet) thick, meant that they could be built only on very solid mounds (ideally rock). Walls often contained small rooms (used as sleeping quarters, latrines, stores and guardrooms). At Dover, the outer ring wall was protected by crenellations (battlements), and the gateway was defended by flanking towers. Dover's keep had four storeys, the royal quarters being on the second floor. Entrances were normally on the first floor, reached by an external staircase, and the only windows were in the upper floors.

— Above —
The Townley Jewel, an 11th-century piece of intricate craftsmanship.

— Above —

The highly-wrought Gloucester candlestick, 45 centimetres (18 inches) tall, is a masterpiece of Romanesque art. An inscription referring to Abbot Peter dates the candlestick, from Gloucester Abbey, to 1107–13, in Henry I's reign.

— Right —

A penny coin depicting William the Conqueror.

When a noble died, his son paid a tax to the king and asked permission to inherit the estate. In 1087, the Conqueror died on campaign in defence of Normandy. He left three sons and two dominions. Normandy was given to the eldest son, Robert; England to William, called 'Rufus' (red) because of his fair hair and florid complexion; the third son, Henry, was left a fortune in silver. The division precipitated a determined struggle between them for each other's land.

Robert, whose lack of height gave him the name Curthose ('Short leggings'), was reputedly lazy and dissolute and his dukedom soon descended into lawlessness. Rufus, by contrast, was as capable and determinedly ruthless as his father. He twice invaded Normandy, whereupon Robert pawned him the duchy in order to join the First Crusade. Barons with lands in both Normandy and England had sworn fealty to each of the Conqueror's sons and were forced to break faith with one or the other when fighting broke out. Odo supported Robert; Lanfranc and the Saxons of England supported Rufus. Odo was banished and joined Robert on the First Crusade, dying on the way.

— Left —

Bronze-gilt figures from a 12th-century pyx, or consecration box, used in church, thought to have belonged to the Knights Templar. The long, pointed shield gave protection down to the legs when riding.

Brothers in Arms

— Left —

Soldiers in Norman battledress, with chain mail, lance and conical helmet. The mail tunic was split for riding.

— Above —

William I hunting, from a 14th–century manuscript. The king apparently loved 'the high harts as he were their very father'. He also 'pulled down towns, villages and churches ... for the space of 30 miles to make thereof a forest ... called the New Forest'. Blinding or death awaited those who poached the king's 'beasts of the forest'.

Normans, like their Viking ancestors, were skilled horsemen who relished the battlefield and the hunting forest. Their warhorse was the destrier, ridden high in a built-up saddle by knights wearing the hauberk, a knee-length shirt of mail, and a conical helmet with projecting nosepiece protecting the head. A long, kite-shaped shield of leather, stretched on a wooden frame, covered the body.

Knights charged almost standing in their long stirrups, a lance held ready to thrust at the enemy. In hand-to-hand fighting, they slashed with a broad-bladed sword. Fighting bishops like Odo wielded the mace, an iron club that felled the enemy yet met the Church's rule that priests should shed no blood.

William Rufus fought to extend Norman authority into south Wales and into northern England, settling Cumberland with southern peasants and refortifying Carlisle, previously under Scottish control. One of many raids by the Scots resulted,

— Above —

The conical metal helmet worn by Norman soldiers was shaped to deflect glancing blows. Plain and serviceable, it was worn over a padded headpiece and a mail hood, or coif. Some helmets also had elongated central strips to protect the nose.

— Right —

The Rufus Stone marks the site near Cadnam in the New Forest where William II was killed while hunting.

— Above —

A medieval artist's view of William Rufus, mortally wounded by an arrow in the New Forest.

in 1093, in the death of King Malcolm, after which Rufus nominated each of Malcolm's three sons to the Scottish throne in turn, as his vassals.

The king cared little for the Church. But, having appointed Anselm as Archbishop of Canterbury, Rufus became embroiled in the Europe-wide tussle between Church and state in the matter of investing priests. He kept Church appointments vacant to appropriate the revenue for himself, while monks condemned with distaste the fashions of his court – long hair, pointed shoes and effeminate behaviour.

Among the king's pleasures was hunting, which kept warriors in training. William I had turned great tracts of land into royal parks for this sport, displacing inhabitants and imposing harsh penalties on those who poached his deer and wild boar. But hunting was also dangerous. In August 1100, as his brother Robert Curthose was returning a hero from the Crusades, William Rufus was killed in the New Forest, shot in the back, apparently by accident. The man blamed, Walter Tirel, fled abroad.

The king's other brother, Henry, also hunting that day, rushed immediately to Winchester where he seized the treasury. Rufus's body was left for peasants to pick up and take by cart to Winchester. There it was buried under the cathedral tower, the authorities being reluctant to grant Church rites.

William Rufus had never married. Three days after his death, Henry was crowned king of England. There is no proof that he had anything to do with Rufus's mysterious end, but he undoubtedly profited from it.

— Right —

The effigy of William the Marshal, Earl of Pembroke (c.1146–1219), in the Temple Church, London. The foremost knight of his time, friend and counsellor of Henry II, William later became regent of England.

Winner Takes All

Robert returned from the Crusades with money to redeem his dukedom but Henry, with a kingdom already secured, had no intention of giving it up. Following a failed invasion of England in 1101, Robert renounced his claim in favour of a pension. Henry then landed in France, defeated and captured his brother at Tinchebrai in 1106 and kept him prisoner in England until his death, aged 80, in 1134. England and Normandy had a single ruler once more.

— RIGHT —
The great seal of Henry I as depicted in a 19th-century engraving.

Henry I's nightmare (1130): the 'three orders' of Norman society – those who prayed, those who fought (below), and those who laboured (above) – appear in the king's dream to protest against high taxes. A further scene features the ship of state tossed in a storm that calms only when the king vows not to collect Danegeld for seven years.

The Norman kingdom was at its largest and most powerful under Henry, the ablest ruler among the Conqueror's sons. Welsh and Scottish kings remained his vassals. Promising good government, he issued a charter of liberties and extended his father's administrative reforms. He issued sealed writs, or letters of royal command; employed travelling justices and sworn juries to inquire into matters of royal concern; and appointed a justiciar as a kind of regent when he was absent in Normandy. Henry

— Below —

Effigy in Gloucester Cathedral of Robert Curthose, Duke of Normandy and son of William the Conqueror. Robert died at Cardiff Castle but was buried in Gloucester, where this memorial was erected in the mid-13th century.

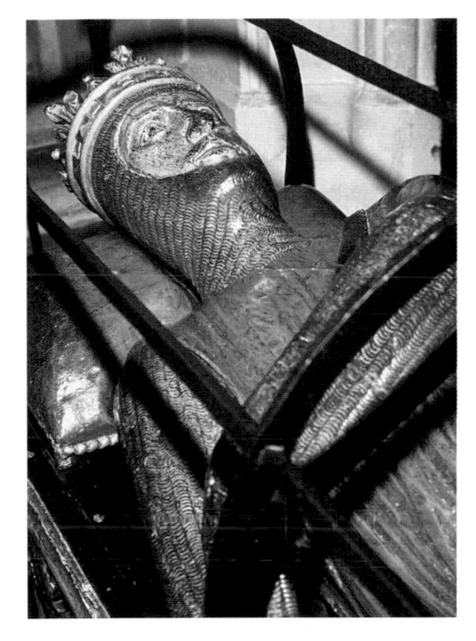

— Above —

The stone keep of Cardiff Castle. A motte with wooden buildings on top was first raised c.*1093, and replaced with stone in the 12th century. Early wooden towers were homes for Norman noblemen and their families but for Robert, Duke of Normandy, the castle was a prison for 28 years.*

also made amends with Anselm and the Church, keeping the homage of the bishops but giving way on the king's right to the spiritual investiture of priests.

Continuing Norman support for monastic reform, Henry received Cistercian monks to England, where they founded Rievaulx and Fountains abbeys in Yorkshire and raised the sheep on which England's future prosperity would be built. The Church also educated those entering the priesthood, government or law, all of which used Latin, although in the late 11th century a certain Master Theobald was instructing between 60 and 100 students at Oxford. Trade and towns grew, especially London, which was granted a charter allowing it to elect its own justices and collect its own customs duties.

Henry also excelled at diplomatic marriage, disposing his 21 illegitimate children (a record for an English king) to produce a ring of favourable alliances. He himself had chosen to marry Matilda, daughter of Malcolm III of Scotland and Queen Margaret, the great granddaughter of the Saxon king Ethelred the Unready.

— Above —

The Jew's House, Lincoln, shows the type of sturdy stone dwelling which might have been occupied by successful 12th-century families of the flourishing merchant class.

Matilda

'Each of his triumphs only made him worry lest he lose what he had gained; therefore though he seemed to be the most fortunate of kings, he was in truth the most miserable.' So said the chronicler Henry of Huntingdon about Henry I.

One of Henry's triumphs had been to marry his 11-year-old daughter Matilda to the German (Holy Roman) Emperor in 1114, a huge dowry of silver bringing her the title of Empress that she used all her life. However it was his son, William, who carried Henry's hopes for the Norman dynasty, and William drowned one cold November night in 1120, crossing the Channel in a ship on which nearly all aboard were drunk. Out of 200 people there was just one survivor.

His first wife having died in 1118, Henry married again, but there were no more children. The nearest male heir, Robert's son, William Clito, was killed in 1128, but Henry had already fixed his ambitions on his daughter Matilda. After her husband's death in 1125 she returned to England, where Henry made his barons swear allegiance to her as heir, in association with 'her lawful husband, should she have one'. And Matilda soon did. He was Geoffrey, Count of Anjou, whom she married in 1128 to disrupt Anjou's alliance with the King of France. She was 26 and he was just 15. Proud and wilful, they soon separated, but were reunited to produce their sons: Henry, in 1133, and Geoffrey a year later.

The Norman nobles, restive at the prospect of a woman as their liege lord, were forced more than once to renew allegiance to Matilda, while the heiress and her husband Geoffrey quarrelled not only between themselves but also with Henry, demanding land, money and castles in characteristic Norman style. Henry himself lived most of the time near his grandchildren in France, where in 1135 he died at a hunting lodge, traditionally of a surfeit of lampreys, but possibly of a heart attack.

With Anjou waging war against Henry, Matilda was met as an invader in Normandy by the nobles who owed her homage. While the barons decided what to do next, Matilda's cousin Stephen took action. Stephen of Blois, son of the Conqueror's daughter Adela, had grown up at his uncle Henry's court. Henry's death was Stephen's chance and he took it.

— Right —

Henry I (top) laments the loss of three of his children, including his heir, William, in the White Ship *(1120). A contemporary account records that Henry's nephew, Stephen of Blois, left the ship before it sailed, feeling ill.*

--- Left ---

The fiery and arrogant Matilda, daughter of Henry I. Though she failed to become queen, through her marriage to Geoffrey of Anjou she bore Henry II, first of the Plantagenet kings of England.

--- Right ---

A portrait in enamel of Geoffrey, Count of Anjou. Nicknamed Plantagenet, he was married to Matilda in 1128 at the age of 15.

--- Above ---

Illustrations from a calendar, c.1120–40, possibly from Worcester Cathedral Priory. Zodiac signs appear beside appropriate tasks for the months of the year.

King versus Empress

Stephen, favourably placed at Boulogne when Henry died, at once crossed the Channel. His lordships in Kent and Essex, on London's trade route with the continent, helped him win the city's crucial support while Winchester, where his brother was bishop, provided him with the treasury. Charming and affable, Stephen persuaded the Archbishop of Canterbury to crown him at Westminster on 22 December 1135.

The barons now had either to support the enthroned king of England, or risk the loss of their English lands by championing Matilda in France. Stephen needed to enforce his authority quickly. But, gallantly brave in warfare, he had not the single-mindedness of the Conqueror and his sons. He also alienated support by humiliating Roger of Salisbury, justiciar of Henry I and controller of the country's administration. Sensing an opportunity, Matilda's half-brother, Robert of Gloucester, took up her cause. When the Empress landed at Arundel in 1139, Norman England faced civil war.

— Above —

King Stephen with a falcon on his wrist, from a 14th-century manuscript. Hawking was enjoyed by both noble men and women.

The Great Hall at Castle Hedingham, Essex (*c.*1140), a favoured residence of Stephen's queen Matilda, who died there in 1152. A castle hall, strewn with rushes or reeds and hung with woollen embroideries, was used for eating, sleeping and business. The baronial family dined at a separate high table and retired to a private curtained area. Others dined at benches (or stood up) and slept on the floor. Later castles had a room, or solar, often at the top of the central keep, for the baron's use.

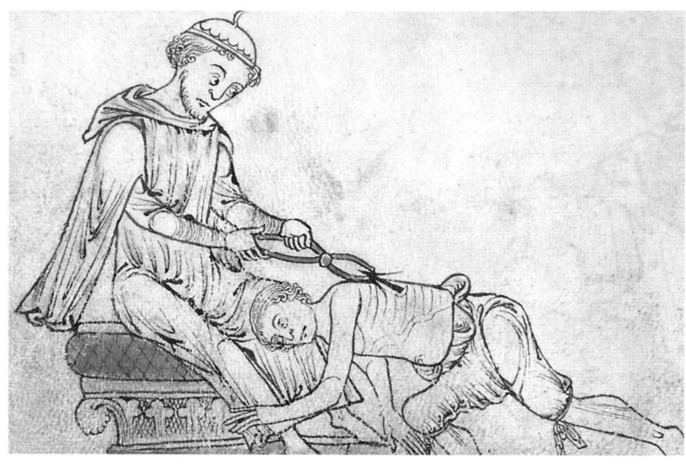

— Left —

Stephen of Blois and his wife, Matilda of Boulogne, appeared on coins struck at York, which remained loyal to the king.

— Above —

Norman medicine was a mixture of folk remedies and ambitious surgical techniques. Care of wounds was a frequent challenge.

The ensuing anarchy lasted until 1154. Chroniclers of the time recorded, 'It was said openly that Christ and his saints were asleep'… 'You could see villages … standing solitary and almost empty because the peasants of both sexes and all ages were dead.' Uncurbed, the barons tasted independence, flouting royal authority, acting lawlessly, some with wanton cruelty and destruction, building unlicensed castles to house private armies. Baronial infighting, which the Norman kings had striven to prevent, now seemed set to destroy the land as towns were burned and plundered.

Neither side seemed strong enough to win. Stephen showed his lack of Norman ruthlessness by letting Matilda slip from his grasp when he had the chance to capture her. By contrast, the Empress's arrogance cost her the kingdom after Stephen's capture at the Battle of Lincoln. Antagonizing potential support by her autocratic demands, London rose against her, as did Winchester, where Robert of Gloucester was captured and later exchanged for Stephen, who resumed the kingship.

Matilda's husband, meanwhile, had been fighting his own battles for Normandy, which he finally gained in 1144. Henry I's Norman empire had fallen apart.

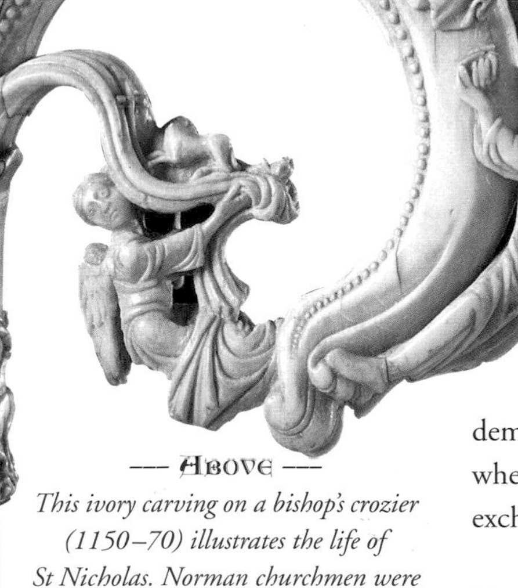

— Above —

This ivory carving on a bishop's crozier (1150–70) illustrates the life of St Nicholas. Norman churchmen were patrons of architecture, learning and art, which became increasingly decorative.

The Norman Legacy

Matilda left England in 1148, never to return. Robert of Gloucester was dead, but the Empress's claim to the throne was kept alive by her young son Henry, who by 1150 was ruling Normandy. When Stephen's son died plundering in East Anglia, a way opened to unite England and Normandy once more. Stephen would adopt Henry as his heir.

Henry II, first Angevin king of England, inherited a country that in some ways resembled England before the Conquest: a country beset by factions. But throughout the civil war, the administrative system moulded by the first three Norman kings held together. Trade flickered on and craft guilds paid their dues. The great fairs, like St Giles' in Winchester, resumed after a while.

— Right —

Decoration typical of the Romanesque style.

— Below —

Henry II on horseback, depicted on the reverse of his royal seal.

— Above —

Holy Sepulchre, Cambridge, the oldest of four round churches in England, was founded in 1130 by the Knights Templar on the model of the Church of the Holy Sepulchre, Jerusalem.

— Left —

The Norman kings of England, from a history by Matthew Paris (1250–9). Each holds a building with which he was connected: William I, Battle Abbey (top left); William II, Westminster Palace hall (top right); Henry I, Reading Abbey (bottom left); and Stephen, Faversham Abbey.

The exchequer kept going and taxes were paid, even though revenues might pour into the local barons' coffers. The justice system survived, as courts met to hear pleas. The Church even benefited, through monastic foundations set up by those needing to atone for wartime misdeeds.

Some nobles escaped from the civil war by joining the Crusades. Knights from England fought for the king of Portugal against the Moors, just as earlier Normans under the Church's banner conquered Sicily while William I established his conquest in England.

That conquest left England, and later the rest of Britain, an enduring legacy of language, law and architecture. The Normans gave fresh energy to the Saxon state, adapting law, government, Church and economy to create an efficient, centralized administration that produced the exchequer and the Domesday Book. They built solid castles and splendid cathedrals; they introduced over half the words currently used in the English language; they kept invaders at bay and drew internal borders that still exist today. Above all, William's victory at Hastings wrenched England away from the Scandinavian world and into the mainstream of European history.

— Above —

The exchequer at work c.1147, as coins are weighed before the king. The exchequer, begun around 1110, was the twice-yearly treasury audit of sheriffs' accounts, at which calculations were made on a 'chequered' cloth.

— Below —

Rochester Castle tower keep dominates the town and the River Medway. The building defied siege and assault by fire, grappling hooks, ladders, rams, stone-throwers, mined tunnels and artillery 'engines'.

Places to Visit

Battle Abbey,
East Sussex: site of the Battle of Hastings.

Bishop's Palace,
Bayeux, northern France: Bayeux Tapestry displayed.

Bury St Edmunds,
Suffolk: Norman tower gateway and church.

Church of the Holy Sepulchre,
Cambridge: rare surviving round church.

Canterbury Cathedral,
Kent: Norman crypt with carvings.

Castle Rising,
Norfolk: early Norman castle and church.

Chepstow Castle,
Monmouthshire.

Chester Cathedral:
former Benedictine abbey.

Chichester Cathedral,
West Sussex: resemblances to St Stephen's, Caen, church of William I.

Colchester Castle,
Essex: Norman keep.

Cormac's Chapel,
Cashel, Tipperary, Ireland: Romanesque church.

Dover Castle,
Kent.

Dunfermline Abbey,
Fife: remains of Benedictine abbey.

Durham Castle and Cathedral:
outstanding example of Norman architecture.

Edinburgh Castle:
St Margaret's Chapel.

Ely Cathedral,
Cambridgeshire: Norman doorways and carvings.

Exeter Cathedral,
Devon: Norman features; Exon Domesday, an early draft of the survey.

Fountains Abbey

Fountains Abbey,
Yorkshire: remains of Cistercian monastery.

Gloucester Cathedral: Norman nave and crypt; tomb of Robert Curthose, Duke of Normandy.

Kilpeck Church,
Herefordshire: well-preserved church, one of the finest in Britain, noted for its carving.

Lincoln:
Norman castle and cathedral (doorways and carvings); Jew's House and other Norman dwellings.

The Tower of London

London:
British Museum; Museum of London; Victoria and Albert Museum; Public Records Office, Kew: Domesday Book; Tower of London: White Tower, built by William I and William II; Westminster Abbey: Norman undercroft of dormitory; Westminster Hall, Houses of Parliament: banqueting hall of William Rufus.

Mellifont Abbey,
Louth, Ireland.

Norwich,
Norfolk: castle, museum and cathedral; Carrow Abbey; marketplace.

Oxford:
castle tower (St George's) and mound; cathedral.

Pembroke Castle,
Dyfed.

Peterborough Cathedral,
Cambridgeshire: fine example of Romanesque architecture.

Pevensey Castle,
East Sussex: Roman fort built on by Normans.

Rochester,
Kent: castle and cathedral.

Romsey Abbey,
Hampshire: Unspoilt Norman church.

Salisbury,
Wiltshire: Old Sarum, remains of Norman cathedral's ground plan.

Tewkesbury Abbey,
Gloucestershire: Romanesque church, tall columns and central tower.

Weald & Downland Museum,
Singleton, West Sussex: reconstructions of domestic buildings.

The Winchester Bible

Winchester,
Hampshire: cathedral, early Norman transepts, Norman font; St Cross Hospital Norman church.

Worcester Cathedral:
Romanesque crypt; circular chapter house.